Accountability
@work

CAROLYN TAYLOR

Accountability
@work

HOW TO MAKE AND KEEP PROMISES
AND HAVE OTHERS DO THE SAME

WALKING
YOUR TALK
PRESS

WALKING YOUR TALK PRESS

https://carolyntaylorculture.com/

First published 2021

A catalogue record for this book is available from the British Library

ISBN: 978-1-8383296-0-0

10 9 8 7 6 5 4 3 2 1

Designed and typeset by Richard Ponsford/www.librodesign.co.uk
Printed and bound in the UK

I want especially to acknowledge Lynn Pearce and Pete Mildenhall for the many hours we spent together building the original models on which this book is based, and Josie Taylor and Rachel Bladon for helping me put this into words. We all knew these principles were changing our lives when we taught ourselves how to apply them. I hope they will have the same effect for you.

CONTENTS

FOREWORD

In 1961, JF Kennedy committed to "achieving the goal, before this decade is out, of landing a man on the moon and returning him safely to the earth." By the end of July 1969, every part of this commitment had been met. Politicians are notorious of course for not keeping their promises, but on this occasion, the promise-making process worked perfectly.

Imagine a world where everyone did what they said they would do, exactly when they said they would do it. Imagine a world where promises were made consciously – and kept. Where you could be confident you could rely on other people to do what they said they would. Think what an impact being a renowned promise-keeper would have on your reputation and your customers' trust of you, and how it might alter the way your business and work relationships function.

This is the transformational quality of a promise made and kept. This is the life-changing power of accountability. Plenty of people talk about accountability. But lip-service accountability will not improve your performance or your reputation.

It doesn't matter how polished the processes are or how brilliant the people – in a business, if accountability is not instilled consistently in a company's culture, their capacity to perform will decrease.

My career as a leadership coach and advisor has allowed me to observe just how many people struggle with this issue at work. They are frustrated with their inability to make things happen in their business, by their lack of ability to get others to do what they said they would do, and by what they see as a lack of commitment and drive from people. And their concerns became even more acute with the arrival of COVID-19 and the "new normal" flexible working conditions. Why has your team under-delivered again, for the third quarter in a row? Why can't your colleague reliably complete the first section of your joint report by Monday so that you can deliver the final document by Wednesday?

What exactly goes on between two people when one person wants the other to do something for them? Is it just a matter of asking? If so, why is it that so many things never get done?

With the help of many colleagues, I've spent years developing a set of principles, behaviours and skills that allows leaders to create a scalable system of accountability based on making and keeping promises. This little book condenses that methodology and gives you the same advantage my colleagues and I offer our clients: a road-map for developing accountability in human beings. Accountability in those on whom you depend; and accountability in yourself, so that you can consistently deliver to others. For you to deliver, you need others to deliver to you, and so the two are inexorably linked.

In an age where screens, emails and texts offer us an opportunity to renege on and renegotiate our promises with little fanfare or discomfort, the phrase "my word is my bond" might sound a little old-fashioned. But there is something timelessly empowering about keeping your word. It makes people want to do business with you. There is always a demand for people who deliver. And becoming a person who keeps their promises raises your own self-esteem, too.

Time and time again, I've seen teams pull together to achieve remarkable things by mastering accountability. I've witnessed entire organisations turn around in a matter of months whilst increasing their profitability, harmony and efficiency. I've watched from the sidelines as previously cynical, uninspired work groups become liberated by the personal and professional fulfilment a culture of honour can bring. And many have told me that what they are now applying at work is actually a universal set of skills and habits that are also useful at home. They have even found a way to have their plumber turn up when they said they would!

This book is about bucking trends and improving our way of life. Its goal is to remove accountability from the "too hard" basket and place it firmly back into the mainstream business sphere – not as a fluffy corporate concept, but as a day-to-day reality.

Carolyn Taylor,
London, February 2021

1

INTRODUCTION

What is accountability?

> **accountable** adjective
> responsible to someone for some action; answerable

Accountability is the ability of one person or group to deliver to the expectations of another. Responsibility on the other hand is more general and not based on this two-way relationship. I can be responsible for running a factory, but accountable to my boss or customers to deliver ten tons of goods by Monday morning. Accountability and responsibility are often used interchangeably because many people have not stopped to explore their full meaning, and so they overlook the precise understanding that can allow both to flourish.

In organisations, leaders often try to build a culture of accountability, because they are frustrated that things do not get done. Many leaders are very good at learning to be accountable themselves – and that characteristic will often lead to promotion – but they sometimes have greater difficulty holding others to account. It's as if they assume everyone will be as accountable as they are. Unfortunately, this is often not the case.

Let's look at an example of accountability in action: I order something from an online retail company. They confirm a delivery date. I pay them. We have a contract and the company is then accountable to deliver. They have made a promise to me. When the date arrives and there is a parcel waiting at home, they have fulfilled their promise.

Because they delivered my order successfully, I have built

trust in them that they will do what they say they will do. Which makes me more likely to place another order in the future.

But how would you feel if you placed your order and the company told you, "We'll give it our best shot, but we can't guarantee your order will be the colour you requested"? Or, what if they agreed on a delivery date, but what you'd ordered never showed up? If either of these things happened, your trust would be eroded, and eventually you would stop shopping with them.

Ordering online and having things delivered looks simple – as far as accountability goes – but there are a lot of risk factors for any company to assess before agreeing to make a promise to you. They need to make sure all the goods they advertise on their website are in stock; that they have adequate warehousing facilities to carry the items; that enough staff are ready to pack the order and to then pick it up from the warehouse for delivery at the agreed time; and, if they subcontract home delivery, that they are confident in the reliability of their delivery partner. They also have to consider all the things that could go wrong with their system and how they might overcome these potential problems and still deliver what they have promised to you. They have refined all of these steps so they can confidently make a commitment.

This one example shows the work that has to go into making promises as an organisation. But even for an individual, every promise takes a high level of commitment, because it has a myriad of dependencies and risks that have to be managed.

Accountability in its purest form is a request from one party: "Can I count on you?" The answer to that question from the other party could be "Yes, you can count on me," or "No, you can't." Once this exchange happens in the affirmative, the relationship of accountability is in place. This play on the word acCOUNTability makes this easy to remember – "Can I COUNT on you?" and "You can COUNT on me" is a great exchange to start using as you build these new habits.

Promises

Promises are at the core of accountability.

The contract that takes place in the "Can I count on you?" / "Yes, you can" exchange is a promise. And the hypothesis I want to explore in this book is that if you start to view all your agreements as promises, things change. Just saying it feels different. The word "accountable" can seem cold. It doesn't conjure up any great depth of feeling – but the word "promise" does. It evokes connotations of honour and virtue; it makes you want to do the right thing.

Try using the word "promise" in your everyday language and business dealings. Then start making promises and keeping them. I guarantee your business life will begin to change.

After the promise you start to see people's true colours. An individual's honour and integrity will be apparent in their capacity to keep their word. If someone didn't make a wise promise, then their reason for giving their word in the first place – if they were doing it to please others, to show off, or to get approval – will become starkly visible.

Meanwhile, in this phase after the commitment, the individual who has kept their promise has an opportunity to grow their reputation within an organisation. Because so many people don't do what they say they are going to do, the individual who consistently does can gain enormous respect and power. Over time, those who don't keep their word will be asked to do less as trust that they will deliver diminishes. When someone makes wise promises and keeps them, they become trusted as a person of honour. The better you get at keeping promises, the less it feels like work, and the more pleasurable it becomes.

The Asker and the Giver

It's a vital yet often overlooked fact that we cannot be accountable alone. Of course, we can be very responsible, work hard, do excellent things and achieve amazing results on our own. But to be genuinely accountable, we must be in a relationship with another person who is holding us to account. In every transaction that invokes accountability, there is one person who asks for a promise, and another who gives one. In this book, we'll call these two roles those of the Asker and the Giver.

Most of us play both of these roles over the course of any given day. Certainly, everyone plays the role of Giver, the one who makes and keeps promises. At work the role of Asker can often be played by a team leader, but it can equally well be played by a colleague who asks a peer for something they need, or by a client asking for a service.

Usually the initiator in this relationship is the Asker – but not always. I might see an opportunity to improve the way our team runs its meetings, and suggest to the team leader that I make a proposal as to how to do that. If my suggestion is accepted, then the accountability contract is set in place.

Creating a culture of honour

A culture of honour is one within which people make and keep promises. Our word becomes our bond.

As a leader, if you are able to create a culture of honour, you cultivate:

- empowerment
- a better and self-sustaining approach
- better performance, as a team and for individuals
- multiple business benefits

Achieving a culture of honour requires a very particular style of leadership. Ordering people around and telling them what to do may create compliance, but it does nothing to trigger the sense of achievement and motivation in others which leads them to make and keep promises. And it won't help you build a more accountable culture around you.

> **honour** noun
> honesty, fairness or integrity in one's actions

I recall working with one team who had missed their targets every quarter for five years in a row. I helped them learn the skill of building a culture based on accountability, where people consistently make and keep promises, and the team very quickly became recognised as performers. Within three months they were hitting targets, and within a year they had become the highest performing team in their company. When teams like this say they will hit a specific performance target, they do. If they say they will launch a new product, or complete an IT upgrade by a certain date, they do. They do not let their customers down, nor their colleagues. It may seem straightforward from the outside, but to achieve this level of consistency requires a very specific set of skills, as well as a different way of thinking.

Promise or intention?

"Am I making a promise or an intention?"

You'd be amazed at how much clarity and peace of mind this simple question can bring to your life. It forces you to fully assess your level of commitment to what is being asked, and you'll notice your mindset shift accordingly. When you promise, a sense of duty and commitment comes to the forefront. For an intention, a feeling of space, possibility and hope.

There are times when you cannot and should not give a promise. In these instances, offer an intention instead. An intention is a commitment to do your best and to put in maximum effort. It doesn't necessarily mean that you won't deliver and, in some cases, you might even surprise yourself and fulfil the request with flying colours. But if you don't feel confident to give a promise at the beginning, then the most honest response you can provide is an intention.

> **promise** noun
> 1. a declaration by a person that something will or will not be done, given, etc.
> 2. an express assurance on which expectation is to be based

> **intention** noun
> a thing intended; an aim or plan

A lot of frustration occurs when the Asker hears a promise given, but the Giver only ever meant it as an intention – if salespeople, for example, consider their part of their sales targets to be an intention, and managers allocate costs assuming they were a promise.

Last week, working from home for the day, I planned to cook dinner and rang to ask my partner what time he'd be home.

"Seven o'clock," he responded.

"Is that a promise or an intention?" I asked.

By asking this question, I was helping him to work out what he needed to do to honour his word. If he made a promise and an important email arrived at 6.30 pm, he'd set it by to respond to the next day. However, if he gave me a seven o'clock intention, he'd probably respond to the email there and then, and possibly arrive home later than seven. As the cook, if it's only an intention, I don't put the spaghetti on until he arrives home, thereby avoiding potential resentment and cold carbonara.

With such clear and agreed expectations in place, communication improves, frustration reduces, trust builds.

Avoiding promises

"If promises involve responsibility and commitment, then why should I promise anything at all? Wouldn't I be better giving an intention all the time, so I don't let anyone down?"

There are people who live this way, skirting through life avoiding promises, but they ultimately lose the trust of those who are close to them. By keeping your promises, you start to build a reputation as someone who is trustworthy and can be counted on when the chips are down. This one skill is likely to keep you employed indefinitely, or, if you are self-employed, it'll take you a long way towards continuous employment. It's a quality and personal ethic which employers, clients and customers find ceaselessly attractive.

How does accountability fit with empowerment?

Many leaders focus on building a more empowered culture in order to motivate their people, create faster responsiveness and generate a more agile approach than that which is possible in a highly-controlled, top-down environment. Empowered individuals, sitting within the context of a broad set of goals, deliver within this range and are not strictly held to account for shorter-term deliverables.

Some argue that, with this as the goal, accountability in the way it is described in this book becomes less needed. I have not found this to be the case. But it is true that in organisations where empowerment is strong, the Asker-Giver relationship shifts on a day-to-day basis to one between peers within a team, or between peers in other teams who depend on one another to fulfil their own commitments. Only someone who works completely in isolation has little or no need for the skills of accountability outlined in this book.

I have also found that even the most "empowered" organisations still have commitments made to shareholders and that, when there is a risk these will not be delivered, they find they need to improve their ability to make and keep promises, and must hold each other to account in order to do this.

The accountability journey

Throughout this book, you'll have the option to follow the accountability journey from either the Asker or the Giver's point of view.

The Asker and the Giver have their own steps, before and after the promise, which, when reduced to a diagram, look like this:

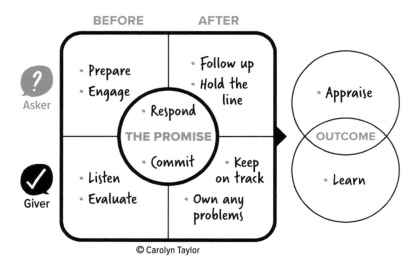

© Carolyn Taylor

The rest of this book will guide you through this accountability journey step by step. I have found time and time again when coaching people in accountability that problems usually occur because earlier steps were not well implemented by both parties. A successfully completed promise requires attention to be paid to each step: the phase before the promise; through the making of the promise itself; the period after the promise as both sides strive to see it implemented; right through to completion, when the promise is fulfilled or not.

BEFORE THE PROMISE

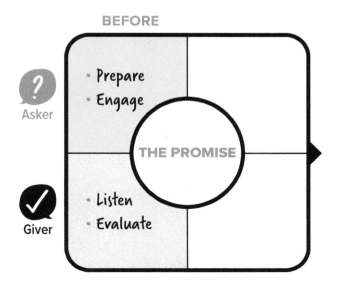

BEFORE

Asker
- Prepare
- Engage

Giver
- Listen
- Evaluate

THE PROMISE

n my experience, the work done before the promise is the most important work of all. It is also the work that is most likely to be missed out. The work done before the promise ensures that when the promise is made, it is a wise one. A wise promise is one which is achievable from the Giver's perspective, and yet contains an acceptable level of stretch from the Asker's perspective.

> Most Givers say "yes" too quickly,
> and most Askers accept that "yes"
> without question because they really
> want what they have asked for.

It is in neither the Asker nor the Giver's interest that a promise is not fulfilled, but the Asker in particular will be left frustrated by any failure of the promise, and will have to deal with the consequences. So the Asker needs to put the work in at this stage to really make sure that his or her request is clear to both parties, and to build confidence that the Giver has done the work to think through and mitigate the risks. The request should be a conversation, a negotiation, and never a one-way instruction from the Asker. The purpose is for the Giver to feel completely bought-in to what is agreed, so that the goal that is promised is fully owned.

 # Prepare

Creating the right relationships and culture

> Achievement motivation is cultivated by a
> series of small, sequential requests which
> build success through a series of wins.

In order to ask for promises from people, and to expect them
to be delivered in full, you first need to establish the kind of
culture in the workplace that enables such a commitment
to be made. As the Asker, your long-term goal is to set up a
relationship of achievement motivation with your Giver – a
relationship which motivates them to achieve everything
they can.

In his research, David McClelland, a Harvard psychologist
(*The Achievement Motive*, New York: Appleton-Century-
Crofts, 1953) found a number of factors which are relevant
to accountability. Everyone has an intrinsic motivation,
McClelland says, a desire to strive and achieve independent
of being forced to do so by others. But this can be severely
curtailed by living in a culture or environment which is
demeaning, or fear-inducing, or "psychologically unsafe"
– a term used by more recent Harvard professor Amy C.
Edmondson (*The Fearless Organization: Creating Psychological
Safety in the Workplace for Learning, Innovation, and Growth*,
Hoboken, NJ: John Wiley & Sons, 2018).

McClelland found that achievement motivation was strongest when people were operating with "self-set goals." When someone feels that a goal has become their own, they are very motivated to achieve it, and they themselves will then do everything they can to anticipate and overcome problems.

On the other hand, if the Giver feels that the goal was imposed on them, they will always blame the Asker in some way if the goal is not achieved. The challenge for the Asker is that there is often a gap between what the Asker wants and what the Giver believes is achievable. Many Askers just see it as the Giver's role to step up to meet their goal. But because it is the Asker who has the more challenging standard, I see it as primarily the Asker's role to find ways to close that gap.

The Asker can close the gap by building over time a relationship of trust, understanding and shared purpose with all of the Givers they intend to work with. In the work environment, this means building a culture within which people feel they can raise difficult issues, have real conversations about what is possible, and be valued for their ideas. Before you get into the specifics of any request, think about the Giver and your relationship with them, and work on improving that. Do you trust this person, and do they trust you? Spend time understanding what is important to them, what motivates them, what their goals are, and how you can help them, in order to create the best possible environment for successful accountability.

Being clear on the request

> The seeds of failure are often
> planted through a poorly planned
> request on the part of the Asker.

I hear a lot of managers complaining about a lack of ownership and accountability from the people who work for them without realising that this admission is as much a criticism of them as a manager as it is of their team.

If you, the Asker, are not clear in your thinking before making a request, then this confusion will become exacerbated once communication with the Giver begins. Sometimes the Giver may not even know you are making a request to them.

Getting clear beforehand about precisely what it is you want will take you a long way towards the delivery of a successful promise. You play a part in successful delivery, and it starts with clarity of request. Sometimes this may mean converting a longer-term goal into a shorter-term specific requested first step. On other occasions, and with certain people, describing the longer-term goal is enough, and can be empowering. But that approach is best when it is taken consciously and deliberately, and still worded as a request.

🔎 CASE STUDY

I recently worked with a company that were introducing a new system of management, known by the acronym PDS. The leader of the company told the organisation that he wanted their full commitment to operating according to the

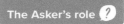

new system. People had long forgotten what PDS stood for, but when this leader asked a group of 50 people whether they were committed to it, everyone nodded in agreement.

Six months later, that same leader was highly frustrated because most people were not following the new system, and in his opinion, they were not being accountable. The employees, when I asked them, said that they thought they were following the system pretty well. What had gone wrong?

The request was too vague: it turned out that "operate according to PDS" meant something different to the Asker than it did to the 50 Givers. By asking people to give their commitment in a large group, any possibility of real discussion about whether this would be do-able had been lost, and the Asker did not encourage that anyway. There was no timeframe given, so six months was in the head of the Asker but not of anyone else. And the goal was probably too big. "Operate according to PDS" turned out to involve a lot of different steps, and needed different interpretation for each of the 50 roles of the people in the room. Because the leader of the company had not planned his request properly, no one had understood it or been able to implement it.

The next time through, the Asker took a different approach. His ask was that everyone read the PDS manual within the next two weeks, and then organise a session within their team run by a trained PDS facilitator, so they could each prepare a plan for how they would implement the system within the next six months. In response to that request, he received 50 "yes" answers, and everyone did what they said they would. And within six months, the system was implemented.

Having planned for his request this time, making it less vague, ensuring that people understood what they were signing up for, and breaking it down into manageable chunks, the leader of the company was able to secure a genuine promise from his staff.

The Asker's pre-promise questions

Before you can utter that all-important request, "Can I count on you?", think through these questions.

1. What is the outcome I am seeking? What do I want to be done?

2. How will I know the promise has been achieved? How will I measure the success of the task?

3. How will I articulate what I'm asking for so that I'm clear? Where could others find ambiguity in what I'm requesting?

4. Who is the best person to get this done for me?

5. What is the Giver's likely reaction to the request? Is it going to be greeted as a challenge, or a chore?

6. Given the nature of the goal, and the competence and experience of the Giver, is this goal best broken down into smaller chunks?

7. Would this request be exciting and motivating for the Giver? Can I adjust it so that it is?

8. How will I deal with any objections the Giver may have to the request? Will I be prepared to revise my request if it seems unlikely to be achieved, or will I help the Giver reassign other current priorities to support this new request?

9. If the Giver isn't willing to commit to a promise, what could be my negotiating position?

23

 **Engage**

The art of asking

The most important part of asking for a promise is to ask.

This may sound obtuse, but it's this vital part, the direct request for a commitment, that is so frequently missing from our exchanges.

People have different reasons for not being good at asking: they are afraid they'll receive a "no"; afraid of conflict; or don't want to be seen as a bother, or needy, or incompetent. Or, as mentioned above, they overestimate the Giver's ability to read their vague messages and act on them, or their interest in doing so.

Whatever the reason, most of us prefer to beat around the bush and do all sorts of things other than just... asking.

🔎 CASE STUDY

A team has spent the day discussing plans for the future and doing a review of how things are going. There are notes scribbled on flip-chart paper or its virtual equivalent. At the end of the meeting, things are rushed and the half hour allocated to "Next Steps" gets cut by 15 minutes. Someone says they will type up the notes, but no date is committed to. The team leader ends by saying what a great meeting it was and how much progress was made, but makes no requests. "We all need to buckle down to make this happen" is the closing remark – a statement, not a request. The leader leaves having false expectations that something is going to happen because she made that statement in front of the others.

A sentence like this isn't a request; it's an assumption. No one has been specifically asked to do anything. By the time an attachment arrives on an email titled "notes from our meeting," assuming they do, a week has passed and everyone has a lot else on their plate. Half the group never open the attachment to the email, and because many did not take notes in the meeting, the things that were discussed are quickly forgotten.

Later, the leader is upset that the team didn't fulfil their promises. Meanwhile, the team members each remain unaware that any request was ever made personally and are left wondering what all the fuss is about.

Just as important as making it clear that you want something is showing that you are making a request and not an order: asking not telling. We all know a few Tellers. Maybe you're one yourself. Tellers are people who set financial targets or deadlines without negotiation, who send emails saying, "Please send me back your thoughts on this by tomorrow," or texts reading, "Pick up this problem for me please. I'm travelling today." It's easy for an Asker to veer into Teller territory, especially if they are in a position of authority.

People do not deliver to a Teller with the same level of accountability as they do to an Asker. Whilst a Teller may believe their demand will generate the result they are seeking, in my experience, telling instead of asking inevitably leads to disappointment and frustration. This is because telling someone what to do does not evoke in them the same level of commitment as that achieved by reaching an agreement with them based on an initial request. A well-negotiated request and promise evokes the Giver's personal sense of honour. It becomes as if the goal was one they had set for themselves. They own it. Telling may achieve compliance, but it does not achieve ownership, except in special situations where the Asker is highly respected by the Giver, and the circumstances demand immediate action.

Asking for a promise: a checklist

1. **Be specific.** Your request must be crystal clear. Include dates, times and measures: "When these notes arrive in your inbox, can you all respond with an email summarising the actions you personally will pick up, with dates, times and deliverables?"

2. **Be persistent.** While children are content to pester a parent until they relent, we adults tend to lack this persistence and will often give up on a request after asking just once or twice. Being persistent means holding on to a vision of what you want and then finding a way to get the other person to agree to it.

3. **Ask the right person.** Make sure that the person you are asking has the ability, authority and control to be able to deliver. If you have planned your request in such a way that it's a comfortably moderate risk for the person, then you'll be better able to stick to your guns while asking.

Commitment conversations

Engaging in conversation is a critical step in getting someone to make a promise to you. Commitment conversations are the to and fro that has to occur between Asker and Giver in order to reach the point of a fully-owned promise. This gives the Asker confidence their request has been understood, and the Giver the opportunity to own their commitment to deliver. When promises are made but not kept, the post-mortem will usually reveal that there was no commitment conversation. Without engagement, the Asker may receive begrudging compliance, but when things start to go wrong, there is blame, justification and a lack of ownership.

The process of asking for the other person's views transforms the act of asking into a commitment conversation.

A commitment conversation is a two-way discussion, not a one-way demand. By involving the other person in the conversation and asking questions like "Do you think that is possible?" or "Can you see any flaws in my thinking?" you start to open up a dialogue which can lead to "What could we do to achieve this?" Through this process, you'll smoke out any doubts, hopefully be able to work together to overcome these, and then transfer ownership of the outcome to the Giver. When you engage the Giver, you may find they help you establish the best solution to the problem, thus reinforcing their sense of ownership.

Just as it can be hard to hear a "no," it is often also challenging for us to listen to other people's doubts. As the Asker of the promise, naturally, we want the other person to respond enthusiastically and without hesitation, and so we're often tempted not to ask hard questions. However, it's in your long-term best interest to meet any concerns head-

on, and early, while the project is still young enough for you to find alternative solutions. You don't want to receive a false "yes" and then "I didn't know what else to say!" three months down the track.

By allowing the Giver to voice any concerns about their ability to fulfil your request and by use of skilful questioning, you are more likely to lead them to the conclusion that they will be able to deliver on the promise. Sometimes, you will need to adjust your request, to make it smaller, but if it gets to that point, it will be because you have exhausted all other options, and you yourself agree that some reduction in the scope of the task is the best course of action if achievement is essential.

Up until now, we've only talked about promises in a pure, singular sense to simplify the concept. However, the individual you are asking to make a promise will more than likely have several active promises on the go at any given time, not to mention their personal goals and commitments. Ask the other person what their priorities look like, so you can zoom out of the discussion and see the bigger picture. Bringing both of your priorities into the conversation means you'll get a more accurate idea of what's possible, not just as an isolated request, but in the context of everything else that's going on.

It's best that commitment conversations are done face-to-face, whether that involves being physically together or on a video call. Many nuances of language and body language are easy to miss without visuals and are almost impossible to gauge through written text. In a situation where many of those who will be Givers to you are not co-located with

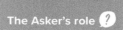

you, but working from home or in other places, your skill at conducting commitment conversations becomes even more crucial, because you are not around to "look over people's shoulders" to see how things are going.

> True empowerment and ultimate delivery
> of outputs is only possible with excellent
> commitment conversations.

To ensure that this engagement stage goes as smoothly as possible, and that every base is covered, it's useful to break a commitment conversation down into a series of steps.

Six key steps in a commitment conversation

Step 1: Clearly state your request or desire.

Step 2: Explain your thinking and reasoning.
"The reason I'm asking for this is…"
"This experience led me to believe you can do this: …"
"I believe that this is an important task because…"
"The benefits for you in doing this will be…"

Step 3: Ask for the Giver's views.
"What's your reaction to what I am saying?"
"Have I been unclear in any way?"
"Do you have any concerns about this?"
"Do you see it differently?"

Step 4: Genuinely listen to their responses.

Step 5: If the ask is a big one, suggest the Giver takes time to work out how this could be achieved.

Step 6: Negotiate to a conclusion depending on their responses.

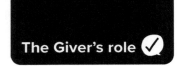
 Listen

Receiving a request

> It usually isn't the process after the promise
> is made that lets people down, it is the
> process beforehand.

When a request is received, it's tempting to respond positively at once. As the Giver, you may find yourself saying something encouraging but a little vague: "Yes, of course," or "I'll try my best," or "Sure." But a vague intention like this is likely to be viewed by the Asker as a firm promise, and to cause big problems down the line.

As soon as you hear a request being made of you, preparation is required. A smart Giver will anticipate a promise that is likely to come, and prepare for it, or better still engage with the Asker to get some advance warning of their thinking. In an organisational setting, for example, Sales will often blame Marketing for not giving them warning of new products or promotions that are coming up. The savvy sales manager will form a close relationship with their peers in Marketing, so they find out what is in the pipeline. If both are part of a close and highly-functioning team, then this will happen through joint planning, but so often I find that groups work in "silos" and do not inform each other of what is going on.

Once a request is made, your preparation starts. Sometimes this only takes seconds as you work through a mental

checklist, but often it needs time. It is unwise to say "yes" to any request before you've had adequate opportunity to think things through. Whilst "Can you meet me for a coffee at 10 am tomorrow?" requires little more than a glance at your calendar and a calculation as to how long it will take for you to get to the agreed venue, a more complex request such as, "Can you deliver this report to me by next Friday at 10 am?" requires time to check things out. And a much broader request for commitment, like, "Can you meet this profit target for the year?" requires a lot more planning, which I will talk about in the next few pages. Unfortunately broad requests like this often arrive as a demand, rather than a request, and so it pays to anticipate their arrival and have plans already thought through.

Don't bow to the pressure of the request in the moment. Take a pause, and respond in a way that affords you more time to do the necessary thinking: "I'll have a look at that and get back to you by 2 pm today. Is that okay?"

Getting clarity

Many requests are delivered in a very vague way. A lot of people are not good at making requests. They hint, they are vague, they talk around the subject. If you want to build a reputation for delivering, ask a question when you hear a vague request. Push for more clarity. This will avoid disappointment later.

Clarity will also enable you to understand exactly what is being asked for.

"I need a response to this email by the end of the week."

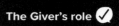
It's rare that two people will have the same understanding of a request like this. What does "the end of the week" mean? Does it mean Friday? If so, what time on Friday? Or does Saturday represent the end of the week for that person? Or even Sunday? And what exactly is the nature of the response requested?

When a request is made, you can mitigate a universe of potential mix-ups by asking questions which help the Asker to be very specific about language. Wherever there is any possibility for ambiguities, ask questions until no more exist.

 Evaluate

Looking at risk

> **risk** noun
> something that creates or suggests a hazard

Before you commit to a promise, as the Giver you need to do a risk assessment of the task, to identify the factors which might prevent you from keeping that promise. People who consistently deliver on promises are skilful at evaluating the level of challenge involved in a task relative to their likelihood of achieving it. They anticipate risk, evaluate its seriousness and mitigate it.

Risks are anything that can happen to cause you to fail to deliver. David McClelland (*The Achieving Society*, Princeton, N.J.: Van Nostrand, 1961) identified risk anticipation and mitigation as one of the key differentiators between people who achieved and others who often did not meet their goals.

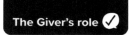
People who have not mastered risk fall into two categories. Some have a "gung-ho" attitude to risk, and their cavalier nature makes them wildly optimistic about what can be achieved, so they operate in the realm of luck, hope and magic, believing something will come along which makes everything possible. Others are so afraid of getting things wrong that they are reluctant to take on anything other than the safest promise.

To be successful at work, you need to find a balance between these two extremes, and be able to stretch and achieve. Continually over-stretching and not achieving will not build you a good reputation, but neither will refusing to take on a request which you feel is demanding in any way. Risk mastery enables you to gradually increase the level of stretch you take on, because you remove the luck, hope and magic, and live in a world where most of what might happen you have anticipated, and mitigated. When completely unexpected things do happen, you are able to quickly swing into gear to address them.

🔎 CASE STUDY

I have promised to give a presentation to a client in the city at 2 pm on Tuesday. Having lived at my address for ten years, I have an intimate understanding of how the traffic flows between my place and the city; all the hotspots, congestion areas and roadworks. I've done the trip so many times, in fact, that I know the range of time it could take me: on a good day, thirty minutes; on a bad day, an hour.

In my initial assessment, I would also consider the reliability of my car, if there is enough petrol in it (or do I

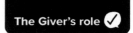

have to stop at the petrol station on the way?), and how much parking will be available at that hour. Are there any major events being held that day that could hinder my journey? I think through as many possible scenarios as I can to accurately gauge when I should leave the house to arrive with enough time to keep my word, look professional and do the best presentation possible. But not so much time that I'll be hanging around for hours beforehand.

If I also need to pick up Paul on my way to the presentation, then another risk is added to the equation. Now I not only have to take into account the route, traffic and journey variables, I also need to consider Paul's reliability. Does he usually run on time, or is he frequently late? What has my experience of Paul been in the past? If I don't know Paul, then this adds a further dimension of risk to the equation.

Now imagine I need to do all of this while my city is hosting an Olympic Games. The city has never experienced a Games before, so no one has any idea how the traffic will be affected. I have no experience to draw upon, just an unknown factor: an unusual event I have no control over. Because my ability to anticipate this risk is almost nil, I'll need to add considerable time to my journey to ensure that even in the worst-case scenario, I will still be able to keep my promise.

Risk anticipation and mitigation solutions usually fit into two categories: reducing the risk of something problematic occurring at all, and having a Plan B for if it does. Detailed risk anticipation and mitigation continues after the promise, but you need to do enough before the promise to increase your confidence that you can commit wisely. In the example above, risk anticipation and mitigation might involve filling

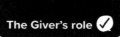

up your car the night before. Plan B might mean having knowledge of alternative forms of transport so you can park and hop on a train if traffic gets very heavy.

Negotiating interdependencies

Accountability is a promise between two people, but what happens when we need to rely on others to help us deliver? Once you start involving other people in your promises, the risk becomes infinitely more complicated.

We all rely on other people to deliver our promises. The problem in many cases is that we tend to assume these people know what we think and want, as if via telepathy. If only life were that simple.

If you are relying on others to help you deliver on your promise, how confident are you that they will deliver themselves? Once you've given your word, the other person is not going to want to hear an excuse which centres around how someone else let you down. So you too must become the Asker.

🔎 CASE STUDY

Say you make a promise to Anna to recommend which segment of the market is going to be the most attractive for focus by the sales team. Anna has asked for this recommendation by the end of the quarter. But to fulfil your promise to her, you will need to secure promises from Bob, Carla and Dan.

Bob has been researching what competitors are doing, and this information is important for your recommendation. Carla is building a new product which,

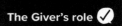

if it comes to market quickly enough, would incline you to recommend a particular segment which will love this product. Dan is in charge of service, and you don't want to recommend a market that he is then not able to support later.

By making this promise, you take responsibility for Bob, Carla and Dan. You can't come back later and say, "I'm sorry Anna, but Dan blew it," because contained within your promise was a pre-assessment of the reliability of Dan to deliver. By promising, you are effectively saying, "I've weighed up all the factors, and I'm of the belief that Bob, Carla and Dan can deliver what I need on time. Therefore, I can make this promise to you."

The fewer people involved, the easier it is to keep a promise, so try to get commitments from individuals, rather than teams who can later blame each other if nothing is delivered. If you are reliant on suppliers to deliver goods for you to keep your promise, see if you can deal with just one person at the supply company. Then ask that person to give you a promise, too. In giving your word, you're backing your judgement of any interdependencies. The buck stops with you.

Negotiating interdependencies: a checklist

1. Who do I have to rely on to make this happen? Who else is involved?

2. What is it that I need them to do?

3. What's my relationship with that person? Will they see doing this for me as a priority and how can I make it more likely that they do?

4. What has been my previous experience with this person?

5. Do they usually keep their word? How can I help them to do so this time?

Assessing other factors

1. Timeframe

What span of time will elapse between the promise and delivery? A promise made for delivery in a year has a far greater risk attached to it than one slated for delivery tomorrow because over a longer timespan many more unexpected, random circumstances can intercept which could jeopardise delivery. Promises with longer timespans can be achieved, but they require a much higher level of skill and commitment to find alternative solutions when these events occur. Making timelines shorter or scaling the promise back to include smaller outcomes one step at a time will increase the likelihood you will keep your word. Sometimes the best negotiating approach with the Asker is to promise the first steps and describe the rest as intentions until you have been able to do more work to see how realistic they are to achieve.

2. Complexity

The less complicated a promise is, the easier it is to keep. Look for ways to cut the frills. It's better to promise to do one straightforward thing than to fail to deliver on a series of complicated things that are all due at once.

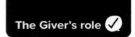
3. Familiarity with the task

If the task is one you have done before, or you know the people who will be involved well, then it is easier for you to make a commitment. Your experience means that you can readily anticipate and mitigate risks. With a task that you are less familiar with, on the other hand, there is more uncertainty for you.

The final decision

Once you've got clarity on what is being asked, completed your planning, anticipated the risks involved and negotiated with those on whom you will be dependent, do you feel ready to make a promise? Only you can judge how much certainty you need to have before you make a promise. You probably only need 70% or 80% certainty, because you do have to depend to some extent on your ability to work through problems that arise along the way. Some may be happy with a much lower level of certainty, say 50%, while others will want it to be much higher. I have found that I have got better at judging this as I have practised the skills of keeping my word, in particular anticipating and mitigating risks, and taking responsibility for fixing problems rather than using them as a justification for non-delivery.

After careful consideration of these factors, you should now be in a position to respond in one of the following ways:

- Make the promise.
- Negotiate a different promise.
- Offer an intention.
- Say no.

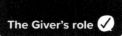

Of course, no one can predict the future. The best you can do as the Giver of a promise is to anticipate as much of the future as you can while using your own knowledge to build adequate contingency for any hurdles you might have to leap over. Those skills are the ones which differentiate those who deliver from those who do not.

THE PROMISE

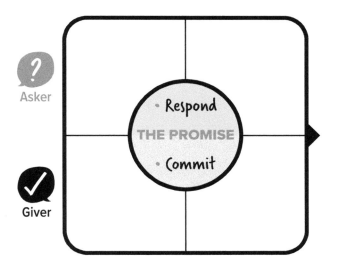

Asker

Giver

- Respond

THE PROMISE

- Commit

The moment comes for a promise. The handshake. The contract. The commitment by the Giver that they will deliver something to the Asker. When all of the work before the promise is done well, this is an uplifting moment, a chance as the Giver to give your word with confidence to an Asker who trusts you and also feels confidence that what is agreed is do-able and meets their needs.

Ideally this is a moment that both parties remember occurring. It becomes the reference point for future discussions about delivery. The worst situation is when this moment never occurs, or occurs in the Asker's mind but not in the Giver's. That is when accountability starts to really suffer, both parties later feel aggrieved and blame the other, and the deliverable itself does not appear. The ultimate beneficiaries of this moment going well are customers, shareholders and other external stakeholders. Equally these groups suffer the most when promises are made in organisations where a culture of accountability has not been established.

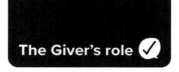

The Giver's role ✓

 **Commit**

Giving your word

When you feel confident that you can give your word, do so clearly and unequivocally. Part of mastering being accountable is to be explicit at this point so that later both you and the Asker will know that you delivered. I like to use the word "promise," and then later, when I fulfil the request, I may say, "Remember I promised to send you through those ideas? Well, here they are."

There are essentially five different ways in which you can respond well to a request. And five ways of responding which immediately position you as someone who is not deliberate enough in giving your word. A good Asker will challenge you if you offer one of the second set of responses.

Acceptable responses

"Yes, you can count on me. I promise to ..."
"No, I cannot be counted on to do that."
"I commit to respond to you by (date)."
"I need clarification."
"I counter-offer ..."

Unacceptable responses

"I'll do my best."
"I'll get back to you."
"Sure, no problem."
"Leave it with me."
"Let me see what I can do."

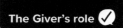

> ### 🔎 CASE STUDY
>
> Some years ago, my company were having to make a major decision about partnering with another firm to go out to clients together with a joint offering. We had searched the market, interviewed and got to know lots of firms, negotiated the commercial arrangements and narrowed it down to a choice of two. Both firms fitted what we wanted, but one of the two stood out from the other with a single differentiator which led to our choosing them.
>
>   Yes, you guessed it. They always kept their word. Throughout the months we spent getting to know each other, they consistently gave their word clearly and unequivocally, having considered our requests of them, and sometimes offered a promise even ahead of our asking for one. The clarity with which they did it gave us confidence immediately, which was then validated by their ability to deliver on their promises. That differentiator led us to choose them as a partner, and resulted in some major financial success for their firm. What they undertook was nothing more than what is described as the Giver's role in this book. The benefits were substantial for them and for us.

Over-promising

There are lots of reasons why people offer a promise glibly. Some people make promises just so that people will like them or to avoid conflict; others make promises because they feel they are being pressured to do so; while others make promises so they can feel important. Many have an overly optimistic view of potential risks.

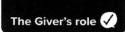

Over-promising is a common mistake that is motivated by a desire to please the Asker. Ironically, this sort of gratifying promise ultimately displeases everyone when what was over-promised is under-delivered. Being honest at the start, and expressing doubts that the request is not possible, is the way to keep the relationship solid and build trust.

> Your long-term reputation is better served by saying "no" than saying "yes" and not delivering.

🔎 CASE STUDY

A team I got to know well had the over-promising gene well established in their culture. They all did it, both to their Head Office when it came to sending in their forecasts, and to their peers – other teams in the organisation who depended on them. They were a team whose customers were other internal departments, although I am sure that if they had had external customers they would have done the same thing. They had simply got into the habit of cheapening the value of their word. They gave it too easily, and broke it with too many excuses.

Why did they do that? I asked them that question, of course. It seemed so obvious to me that they were shooting themselves in the foot, doing themselves a lot of damage, both individually and collectively. Their answers were varied. Some, when they were really honest with themselves and with me, admitted that they did it because they wanted to impress. They had a show-off energy – they over-estimated their own ability, and liked to make out that they were heroes, capable of

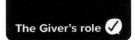

overcoming any obstacle. Others admitted that they felt pressured, especially by Head Office, and were afraid to push back.

By over-promising and then not delivering, they had ended up with a bad reputation, and had become flagged as non-performers. Yet it was surprisingly difficult to help them to overcome their instinctive tendency to over-promise.

Making a counter-offer

If, after weighing up the risks, you reach the conclusion that you can't guarantee delivery of what is being asked of you, then renegotiation is the best course of action.

In most circumstances, just saying, "No, I can't do that" is not the outcome you want, and you will not last long in an organisation if you do this often. Who wants to build a reputation for being the person who says "no," when you probably live in a "can-do" culture? That's why learning how to negotiate an agreement that works for both parties, and which you can promise to deliver, is an essential skill.

Think carefully: What do you feel you *can* promise? Suggest this as an alternative. You can still offer to *intend* to deliver more, but let the Asker know that you can't promise because there are too many factors standing in the way. Distinguish between promise and intention.

Sometimes, reducing the size of the promise is acceptable:

"At this stage, I can't promise you $100,000 by the end of December for these reasons ... I'll certainly give it my best, but I'm

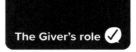

not confident enough to be able to make a promise to you today. However, what I can promise you right now is $40,000 by the end of September. We can then review our position at the end of September and re-evaluate for the final quarter."

You can also make a promise which is conditional on something else being sacrificed:

"I can deliver those website mock-ups for you, but it will mean delaying the new logo design. Is that acceptable to you?"

Or you can ask for help to deliver the promise:

"I can pick up the work of this person who has resigned, and still deliver on my own numbers, but only if I have some extra resource. Are you okay if I hire a contractor for three months?"

Your counter-offer may be accepted, or the Asker may want to discuss it further. They may push you. But remember, in the end, it isn't in either of your best interests if what is being asked for is not delivered. Try to offer a variety of different workarounds until you find one which is acceptable to you both. Be persistent. Taking the time to get this right now will result in mutual happiness further down the track when the promise is delivered successfully.

⊕ Respond

Dealing with a refusal

In an organisational context, leaders do not like hearing a "no" in response to their requests. So most people say "yes" out of fear that they will be seen as lacking a sense of commitment if they question what they have been asked for. When someone does have the courage to question your request (or demand), I think it is unwise to ignore this. You may consider that others, in the Giver's position, would be able to promise and then deliver. And you may be right. If this is the conclusion you reach, then over time you probably need to find other Givers to work with. But it could also be possible that you are making unachievable demands. And it is better to know that now than later, when the promise is not met and you yourself are in trouble.

Some askers suspect that a Giver is "sandbagging", being overly conservative to avoid failure later on. If this is the case you will have to push for more stretch, but it is how you do it that really matters.

If you spend time building a trusting and psychologically safe environment where people feel they can speak up, then you have the opportunity to resolve these problems together with your Givers, coaching them so that they are able to stretch further than they thought possible, or providing resources or ideas which help them to achieve. Or together you may be able to find a different approach which comes close enough to meeting your needs.

Accepting a counter-offer

There are occasions when you will decide that the safest way
to move forward is to accept a counter-offer from the Giver.
As the Asker, you have your own reputation to consider, and
you will probably be making commitments to other people
based on the assumption that your Giver is going to deliver.
Every leader is held accountable themselves for what they
deliver, and what they deliver is to a large extent the sum
total of what their team provides. If your team members
fail to deliver, your own performance will be impacted. As
a customer, it is often better to hear the truth from one of
your suppliers, and to work around that, rather than assume
you will get what you asked for, and then be let down. On
the other hand, if you accept a counter--offer too easily, then
perhaps your Giver will not stretch themselves to deliver
to their absolute capacity. Or perhaps they will prioritise
other Askers who are less demanding than you. It's a tough
judgement call to make.

In organisations I find the more usual approach is for
leaders to demand that their asks are met, and to not accept
counter-offers. But I have also found that many of those
leaders do not then get the results they demanded. And
in the process they set up a culture where there is a lot of
telling and demanding, but no more delivering, which is
not an environment that produces the best possible results.
If you can build a culture where people are involved in the
commitments they make, have high ownership of them, but
also know that not delivering is then really not acceptable,
over time you build to more consistent delivery of results.

49

Final check

Even when you get a "yes" in response to a request, there is work for you to do. As the Asker, it's your responsibility to make sure that you are receiving quality promises. If you feel that a promise has been given glibly, that it has no substance, or if you have your doubts about its delivery, don't accept it. Question, probe and converse until you're confident you are receiving a promise that has been considered wisely. How much you do this depends a lot on how well you know the Giver and their capacity, capability and trustworthiness to deliver on their word.

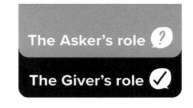

The Asker's role ?

The Giver's role ✓

 # THE PROMISE MOMENT

The moment that a true commitment is given is an important one. If everything up to this point has been done well, both parties should be comfortable with what has been agreed. This moment should be marked in some way that makes it memorable: a handshake, or eye contact, a specific confirmation by email, or some other form of written note if the promise is of an appropriate scale. If the moment is memorable, it becomes easy to refer back to it during the delivery stages which occur after the promise.

At the point of promise, use the language of accountability: *"Can I count on you?"* *"You can count on me."*

Using words like this may feel awkward, but they can symbolise a deeper level of commitment than most people are used to giving. They are the moment where the acCOUNTability contract is entered into.

The Asker: *"Can I count on you to* (define promise and how it will be measured)?*"*

The Giver: *"Yes, you can count on me to* (define promise and how it will be measured).*"*

4
AFTER THE PROMISE

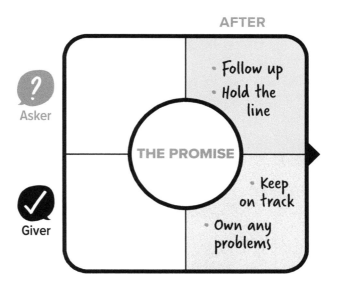

AFTER

- Follow up
- Hold the line

? Asker

THE PROMISE

✓ Giver

- Keep on track
- Own any problems

Just because a promise has been made, that does not guarantee that it will be delivered. Not everyone is a person of honour, after all. Although getting better at the process of agreeing on a wise promise increases the likelihood of delivery, there are still things that need to be done to ensure that a promise reaches the finishing line. Both the Asker and the Giver retain responsibility for ensuring what was promised is delivered. Circumstances change, new challenges and priorities arrive on the scene, and both the Giver and the Asker need to be aware of these and stay focused on what it will take to still deliver, or, on the occasions where that looks less and less likely, to anticipate this early so damage can be limited.

The Asker's role ?

Follow up

Keeping score

Helping the Giver to land a promise that was made to you requires discipline and putting in place habits and processes that make following up routine. Often, as the Asker, your own integrity will be on the line because what was promised to you forms part of a broader promise you have made, perhaps to your boss, so "keeping score" is vital.

The act of keeping score works as a tracking mechanism, a sort of "promise GPS" that tells you how close someone is to where they said they were going to be, or if they've gone off track. If there's no method for keeping score in place, then no one will know what the track looks like, let alone whether they've gone off it or not!

If defining the promise is like drawing the lines on the tennis court, then being able to keep score is the umpire and electronic line judge deciding whether the ball is in or out. Without this mechanism in place, the lines on the court have no meaning.

One of the significant benefits of keeping score is that you can only ever answer a question regarding delivery with either, "Yes, I did," or "No, I didn't." There's no "almost" in a game of tennis: the ball is either in or out. If the ball is out several times in a row, then you lose that game. If you lose consecutive games, then you lose the set, and if this trend continues, you lose the match.

To keep a clear picture of whether a promise is being kept, you need to have an accurate measurement system in place, just as you do on the tennis court. You should always be asking yourself the question, "What evidence do I need to know/give that the promise is being kept?"

The art of following up

1. Know your Giver

In considering how involved you want to be during the period between the promise being made and delivered, you need to draw on your experience of the Giver in other circumstances.

> ### Criteria for knowing your Giver
>
> **100% reliable:** some people are so trustworthy that you know that their word will truly be their bond and what they promised will be delivered exactly as you both agreed, no matter what challenges occur in the interval.
>
> **Mostly reliable:** others you can support to secure the outcome you need by providing more regular contact and sometimes offering ideas and the opportunity to check together whether things are on track. Positive feedback and encouragement will keep your request top-of-mind amongst everything else this person has on their plate.
>
> **Unreliable:** a few people need fairly strong pressure and follow-up because they have a reputation for not doing what they say they will.

If someone considers any form of follow-up to be an insult because they pride themselves on delivering on time and always follow through, and if you are aiming for a culture of empowerment, you need to be very careful or your Giver will become irritated and you will end up eroding accountability. With someone like this, almost no touch points may be the best approach. But with others who are less organised and not so reliable, you do need to do more. Given the tendency for those people to get defensive, it works well to make follow-up a routine that is agreed at the time the promise is made, so that when it happens it is not seen as an attack, but rather part of the normal relationship between the two of you. Over time, you will begin to sense who the people are that you need to stay in closer contact with.

2. Create an approximate timeline

If the delivery date you negotiated in the promise conversation is more than a few days away, then you may need to check to see if the person is on track. If it is a long-term promise, then it's best to break the task down into sections and establish milestones along the way. This will enable you to track progress and help with course correction if necessary. Don't make the mistake of leaving it too long before following up. The longer you wait, the harder it will be to correct any problems in time for delivery.

3. Schedule appropriate and timely follow-up sessions

Unless you are completely confident the Giver will deliver no matter what, create a schedule of appropriate and timely follow-up sessions with the person who has made the promise to you. Involve them in the process. Use your judgement to establish how much follow-up is required, what type of follow-up is best, and how frequently you're going to do it. You can suggest that once a month or once a week you meet or speak to discuss what has been completed and whether there are any anticipated roadblocks which might cause difficulties with meeting the promise later down the track. These checkpoints are an opportunity to solve problems, as well as to celebrate what's been completed and make sure that both you and the Giver are satisfied that everything is on course. Keep the pressure on before the final deadline for a deliverable, or ahead of a final financial goal being met. This gives you the opportunity to coach, redirect and help the other person reprioritise.

🔎 CASE STUDY

You are expecting details of a new product which you intend to offer to your clients, and are depending on its arrival to meet your sales targets. The delivery date was agreed between you and the product people in a "commitment conversation" two months ago. It is in four months' time. If the product is delivered late, you will have to really scramble to find other ways to close the gap in your sales numbers. The more notice you have that the product is late, the more chance you have of filling this gap, and thus fulfilling the promise you have made to your boss. You could set up a meeting once a month with the product people who had agreed to the release date for the product. Here you could check whether they are still expecting to meet the delivery date agreed, listen to their progress, ask if there is anything you can do to help, and find out if there could be a partial release earlier. You can also talk about the risks to the whole company if sales are not met.

Lastly, let the Giver know that you will be following up. Managing culture is all about sending signals that tell people "the way we do things around here." By letting people know you care about follow-up, you're sending a signal that you're serious about promises.

Hold the line

Almost inevitably, things will happen that get in the way of people delivering their promises. It is how well you choose to handle these unexpected events that will determine whether the promise is delivered to you or not, and how successful you are at maintaining a relationship that will help you and the Giver get better at working together to produce the outcomes you both want.

Standing firm

If you're going to be reasonable at any point during the accountability process, then the time to do it is before the promise, during the negotiation phase, not after. Most people operate in the opposite way. They're very unreasonable at the time of negotiation – setting colossal targets and demands of others – and then go weak during the delivery process when their goals are not met. If you have set fair demands, and allowed the promise-giver a sense of choice and the opportunity to negotiate or say "no" to what you were asking for, then they have knowingly stepped up to the plate and accepted the challenge. And as the Asker, you have therefore earned the right to hold your ground.

This is the phase that many people find the most challenging. When things are off track, and the Giver of a promise starts going into justification, blame, denial and defence, your response will influence the outcome. The more you falter and buy into their arguments, the more you surrender the possibility of that person coming up with an innovative, alternative way of achieving the same goal.

Giving positive feedback where possible

People deliver best to those who they like and respect and enjoy working for. In every organisation everyone has a lot on their plate, and many people feel stressed and find it hard to prioritise. Within this context, you want your request and the promise that was made to you to remain top of your Giver's mind. Showing support and appreciation for what they are achieving, and have already delivered to you in the past, establishes the relationship in a way that makes your intention to hold them to their promises more palatable. Empathy for their workload is appropriate, acceptance that this is an excuse for not being accountable for promises they have made is not. This is a fine line to tread, and one which is easier the more you build a trusting and respectful relationship with each other.

The power of creative correction

One of the most significant differences between an intention and a promise is that the latter has an accountability contract built in. If, after the promise, the Giver did not anticipate risks adequately and is finding it hard to deliver, then the fact that a full engaging conversation happened before the promise, and the Giver gave their word, makes all the difference. A Giver who feels they truly gave their word is much more likely to look for and find a new and different way to still ensure delivery, if and when problems come up. By holding fast to a promise and saying, "I'm not prepared to take the heat off that one," you compel that individual to be more creative. You don't have to be unpleasant about it, just stand your ground and say, "A promise is a promise. This is what you told me you could do. Please go back and find a way."

> Don't buy into excuses, but rather, focus on helping the Giver find solutions.

Ideally, solutions will come from the Giver. But in many Asker-Giver relationships, especially the one between a leader and members of their team, the Asker also has the role of coach, and can help the Giver come up with solutions. If you are in the leader role as the Asker though, try to resist the temptation to do the work yourself. Beyond getting the promise delivered, you also have a role to build the capability of your people to deliver and learn to keep promises, and taking the work back does not achieve that.

Sometimes the Giver can get stuck in a narrow set of assumptions, and just works harder and harder to try and deliver. As the Asker, you can help the Giver by encouraging out-of-the-box solutions. "Imagine you had to deliver double what you have promised. What would you do then?" is a great question to get people thinking along completely different lines, because there will most likely be no way they can achieve double by just working harder at what they are already doing.

🔍 CASE STUDY

Imagine a Giver has promised to deliver to you in three months a set of documentation to support a new process that your organisation is introducing. They are running behind and it looks as if it will take them four months, so they are working harder and harder to get everything written. But what if you, as the Asker/coach, suggest that they go to the end-users of that process, the ones who will be reading and following the documents they have to prepare.

Following your suggestion, the Giver might sit down and ask the end-users exactly what they are doing now, and what they will need in the future, and discover that half of what they were going to write is superfluous, because parts of the process duplicate what the users are already doing. The Giver made an assumption, committed to three months, is running behind and working hard to deliver. But in one move, by going to talk to a group of people they had not interrogated, and by asking questions no one had asked, they might find that they can halve their delivery time.

So stay involved, ask good questions, keep the heat on but at the same time be supportive and offer coaching. One of the reasons people don't like to implement follow-up when they are in the Asker role is because they are concerned about the possibility of having to apply consequences, and the difficult conversations that will involve. Everyone usually prefers to cough and splutter, get on with their lives, and let each other off the hook, but I invite you to challenge the status quo. Hold your ground. Once a promise has been made to you, expect delivery of that promise, no matter what. A high achiever would expect nothing less.

Dealing with "reasonable reasons"

When you become serious about promises, you'll start
to notice a very curious behaviour in those around you:
wriggling. Not only will people try to wriggle their way out
of making a promise to you in the first place; but if you
do manage to secure a promise, they start to find excuses
when the going gets tough. Wriggling will usually occur in
direct proportion to the complexity of the promise. A simple
promise is hard to try to wriggle out of, whereas a more
sophisticated promise will give all sorts of opportunities for
justification as to why, for reasons which are always outside
of the Giver's control, it will now not be possible to deliver.

When you encounter "wriggling moments" like these, you'll
usually hear a persuasive chorus of what I call "reasonable
reasons," which all have one purpose: to exonerate.

"Reasonable reasons" are the justifications people provide for
why something won't or can't be done. That doesn't mean
"reasonable reasons" aren't true: they usually are. Here are
some common "reasonable reasons":

*"The competition has launched a better product than ours."/"I have
been given a whole lot more work by someone else."/"I have been
sick."/"The other department did not send through what I needed to
get the work done."*

Of course, there are some "reasonable reasons" that you
will consider really are reasonable, and that could not have
been anticipated, for example, illness or a bereavement, and
in these situations you will therefore accept a renegotiation
of the promise. But even in these circumstances, when the

immediate event is passed, it would be appropriate to suggest that having contingency plans in place for covering such eventualities would be a valuable way of mitigating such problems in the future.

> ### 🔎 CASE STUDY
>
> Not long ago, I was working with a group who provided engineering advice to their clients. They had recently lost an important contract, and the reason given by the client was that they continually missed deadlines. When the leader asked the account manager why that was, the response was, "The client was always late giving us the information we needed to prepare our advice." So it was the client's fault. Now, it may very well have been true that the client did not provide information in a timely matter. So this is a very "reasonable reason," and as the Asker it would be easy to respond by saying, "Oh that's tough, I understand then, you are in an impossible position." But this leader did not do that. She considered that it was the account manager's responsibility to solve that problem when it started to occur. Either to raise it successfully with the client, or to escalate to others in the client organisation, or to let the client know early on that this was going to impact the delivery date. All of those things could have changed the situation and allowed a promise to still be fulfilled.

As an Asker, if someone has given you their word, you have every right to expect it will be kept. When dealing with "reasonable reasons," you will always get what you settle for, so don't give in or give up on what you want. If you settle for an excuse, then you'll have to settle for results that are less than you wanted or expected. Sometimes, that is the only option. You may conclude that no matter how much the Giver takes responsibility for finding a solution, there just is not going to be a way around the problem within the timeframe of the promise. These situations occur. But there may still be opportunities to learn for next time, to put contingency plans in place so that if the situation arises again you and your Giver will be in a better position to respond.

The COVID-19 pandemic, for example, is a circumstance which caused many promises to be broken by individuals and by organisations. Could organisations and governments have anticipated it? Yes – public health experts had been warning for years of the danger of a global pandemic. But many did not anticipate it. They learnt from the experience, but often not enough nor fast enough to maintain promises already made. Others were able to pivot fast and keep themselves on track. Those who learnt fastest were those who did not use the pandemic as a "reasonable reason" but instead came up with innovative ways to still keep their promises to customers.

Questions to someone citing "reasonable reasons"

1. Given X (the barrier or difficult outside circumstance), what can you do to make sure that this project/task is still delivered/accomplished on time?

2. What are the alternative courses of action available to you?

3. What have you learnt from what has occurred, and how will it affect what you do next time?

4. What are the risk mitigation strategies available to you?

Appealing to honour

You can gently remind someone that they gave their word, and to break that reduces their trustworthiness and their sense of honour. You want the other person to keep their word because they want to, because it will increase their own sense of worth and of being a reliable, honourable person. This motive is more powerful and produces more consistent reliability than the motive of doing something in order to get a reward, or out of fear.

> Intrinsic motivation delivers
> even when no one is looking.

Transparency is important in keeping the pressure on. No justifications or "reasonable reasons," just facts. When you thank someone for keeping their word or have a difficult conversation with them about not keeping their word, you are building intrinsic motivation, through pride or regret, in that person.

In a team environment, the transparent presentation of reports which show the status of various promises has the impact of increasing peer pressure to deliver. Everyone wants their commitments to show up with a green rather than a red symbol beside them, indicating they are on track.

Renegotiating the promise

From time to time you'll be given a reason for a delay or problem with keeping a promise that you believe is valid and you'll need to renegotiate. If this occurs, then ask yourself the question: "Have I done all that I absolutely can to overcome this problem?"

If you want to accept the reason and can honestly say that you have explored all avenues to facilitate the fulfilment of the promise, then go ahead and renegotiate. But try to learn from the experience. Ask yourself, "What went wrong here, and what can I do to ensure it won't happen again?"

If you find that you have to renegotiate a promise, you'll probably discover something missing in the planning phase, or an outcome that wasn't allowed for in the Giver's risk anticipation and mitigation. As you develop your skills in negotiating with a Giver, you'll find that you need to renegotiate less. More of your bases will be covered, and you'll be able to hold the line with the knowledge that a promise can be delivered.

When a new promise is offered to you, the cycle of the promise starts again, and you'll need to negotiate with the Giver until you have a promise you are comfortable with. The promise contract begins when you both reach this point.

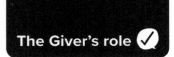

Keep on track

Planning your actions

Most activities are best done if you've planned in advance
how they'll take place. If your promise is a small one,
planning will take place in your head and might take a few
minutes. If the promise is large and extends over a long
period of time, your planning will need to be deeper and more
thorough.

Write down your intended actions. Really take some time,
either alone or with others, to figure out exactly what it
will take for you to fulfil the promise. Perhaps your plan is
no more than scheduling some time in your calendar that
you're going to keep free for a key task associated with your
promise. This works if you have promised a client a proposal
by a particular day, for example. If your promise involves
delivering a revenue number some months down the track,
then your plan will be much more detailed. Either way, you
need something tangible that you can check your progress
against.

Risk anticipation

> **anticipation** noun
> realising something beforehand; foreseeing

Good risk anticipation is an essential skill for keeping your
word throughout the fulfilment of the accountability contract.
If you've already followed the proper planning process in the

first half of this book, then you'll have done your homework already and you'll have identified some of the risks associated with the promise you've made.

We're defining risk in the broadest possible way here, meaning anything which could happen which would jeopardise your ability to meet your promise. It's much easier to mitigate risks if you anticipate them ahead of time. If you haven't, then you could find yourself scrambling for solutions. Some risks can't be anticipated, others can.

Risk anticipation is as simple as sitting down for a moment, or a day, depending on the size of your problem, and asking: "What could occur which would put this promise in jeopardy? What could I do to minimise the impact?"

Risk mitigation

> **mitigation** noun
> making something less severe

1. Reducing risk

In the process of planning your path towards delivering on the promise, look for any critical moments and make alternative plans to deal with them in advance.

> **🔎 CASE STUDY**
>
> Let's imagine one of your designers has been nominated for a major international award and you calculate her odds of winning are one in five. You need her to complete her part of a project you have given a promise for but, if she wins the award, she'll have to travel to San

Francisco to collect it. The awards ceremony is slap-bang in the middle of your project and could severely impact completion and delivery of the promise you have given to the Asker. Even if you had a Plan B stand-in designer waiting in the wings, you might lose style continuity by changing designers. Rather than take the risk of this happening, you circumvent it by employing another designer from the project's outset.

2. Building a Plan B

Some situations warrant a plan which you only put in place if the anticipated risk actually occurs, rather than ahead of time. For example, at the onset of the COVID-19 pandemic, some organisations were able to quickly change their business model because they had already anticipated how they would operate if their people had to start working from home. They might have had plans in place anticipating something different like a major strike on the transport system, but they had done the thinking and put in place the basics. Others had no Plan B, and so were less nimble in their ability to pivot to ensure business continuity.

🔎 CASE STUDY

A company offering training and team-building services to their clients had decided some years ago that they would reduce their risk of being highly dependent on face-to-face delivery of their service to teams who came together for a couple of days in some hotel or workshop facility. They branched out into virtual facilitation, which was cheaper for their clients because there was no travel involved, and meant that they could pull together international teams virtually very easily. Over several years this consulting company mastered virtual team-building, where others thought it was impossible. By having both a Plan A and a Plan B, the company had reduced the risk of not being able to fulfil promises made to clients and to shareholders. When COVID-19 arrived, they were able to quickly swing into 100% virtual delivery, and their clients, keen for ways to keep employees engaged during Lockdown, responded with gusto.

If you think there is a situation likely to arise that will be a hurdle to you crossing the finish line with your promise, then you can decide – at the very beginning – to reduce the impact of this possibility from the process with a Plan B.

Proactive prioritisation

After the agreement has been made, other requests will inevitably appear that could potentially render you unable to deliver on the original promise. You may say "yes" to these without thinking through the consequences, or feel that you have no choice but to take on the extra load. As the situation escalates, it can be easy to feel out of control and overwhelmed. What typically happens is that people try to prioritise their activities instead of their goals, and this is what can lead to a feeling of being "swamped." There are so many potential activities that when you try to order them in a list, it feels almost impossible.

Once you attain clarity about what's important to you, prioritising becomes very simple.

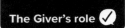

Your list of goals might look like this:

- *Promise to your boss to meet this month's production numbers.*

- *Promise to attend a safety training programme which will take your team out for two days.*

- *Promise to another part of the business that you will deliver some reports on maintenance for an efficiency analysis they are doing.*

- *Self-initiated goal to plan for how to cope with an anticipated shut-down in three months' time.*

- *Promise to your family to get home an hour early all week, because your partner is attending evening degree classes.*

If as you do this, you realise that you have now given more promises than you can fulfil, you will have to choose which Askers you will need to go back to with a view to renegotiating. But before you move to that step, be sure that you have not narrowed your thinking and missed ways to do all of these things. In the next section is a tool which will help you feel more in control and less at the effect of decisions made by others.

Own any problems

Going above the line

"Sorry I'm late, the traffic (or public transport) was terrible."

It's the common excuse for arriving late to a morning meeting. Notice how it blames an external event instead of the tardy individual. Think of this as going "below the line."

When someone goes below the line, they will blame external events or people for their miscalculation. This kind of thinking creates a victim mentality and renders one helpless. It is not a mindset conducive to creative solutions.

Going "above the line," on the other hand, makes you at cause rather than at the effect of traffic and requires a different kind of language:

"I didn't anticipate that the traffic would be so bad."

This sentence places the responsibility for the anticipation and planning of the journey on the individual. You have 100% responsibility for how you respond to the traffic in your city.

To keep promises requires responsibility for outcomes regardless of external factors. The focus is on finding a solution rather than the pursuit of who or what is to blame. People below the line will favour pronouns such as "you," "they" or "it," whereas the language of someone above the line will be "I" and "we"-centred.

We all go below the line from time to time. But how long you stay there and how quickly you correct course depend on you taking responsibility.

🔎 CASE STUDY

Monica had made a promise to her manager to achieve a certain number of sales figures within three months. But a month down the track, those figures were off target.

Her below-the-line responses to this situation were typical of ones you will have heard in your organisation: "They weren't the correct sales figures in the first place,

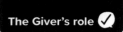
they were forced on me," (thereby assigning blame) or "I was talking with a competitor, and they're even worse off" (justification). Sometimes, she blamed some other department for being off track: "The marketing people didn't execute the campaign on time."

These below-the-line responses framed her as a victim – someone who was in no position to find a dynamic solution. Nothing changed over the next two months, and the sales target was indeed not met.

Luis had an identical target, and was also tracking down at the one-month mark. He took an above-the-line approach. "I didn't work hard enough with Marketing to explain why it was so crucial to my sales that we get the campaign out on time," he said to himself. His next logical move was then to think, "I need to call Marketing right now to see if there is a way we can get this back on track." He made the call, they found a solution, and he was able to speak to his clients with a ready date for the new products, and get them to agree to pre-orders.

Going above the line puts you in the driver's seat. When you use phrases such as "I didn't anticipate" or "I didn't foresee," it suggests that you have the power to fix things, rather than being a helpless victim of external events.

> A characteristic of high achievers is that they see themselves as part of the cause of what happens rather than just being at its mercy.

Going below the line is passive: life happens to you rather than you influencing it. High achievers go above the line:

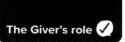

there's not much in their lives that they hand over to luck, chance, magic or external forces.

Making a new promise

Sometimes, a circumstance occurs that you can't find a creative solution for, and as a result, the promise you've given cannot be fulfilled. When you realise this, you need to find and make a revised promise with the Asker.

Under most circumstances, the Asker will still want you to deliver the best you can. So this means offering an alternative promise. Either a later date, a different scope or a commitment that something that occurred will not happen again. Ahead of alerting the Asker to the difficulties in delivering the promise, think through what your new offer is and bring it to the table. It needs to meet all the criteria of any promise in terms of clarity and do-ability.

Don't avoid having a conversation with the Asker to avoid conflict, because this actually causes more damage. Not only do you build a reputation as someone who does not keep their word, you also become known as someone who does not take responsibility for a promise not kept. The second, in most people's eyes, is a much more serious offence than the first.

Your honour is at stake here. In the best case, you would build your honour by keeping your word, but in lieu of this, the next best thing you can do is remain honest, courageous and humble. Show that you're a learner by pro-actively asking to renegotiate your promise and owning the reasons the original promise was not fulfilled.

THE OUTCOME

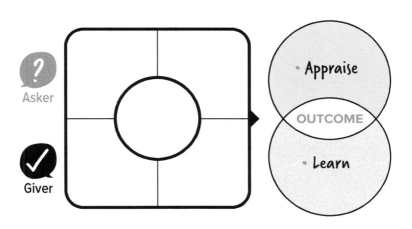

- Asker
- Giver
- Appraise
- OUTCOME
- Learn

> **consequence** noun
> the effect, result or outcome of something occurring earlier

Every outcome has a consequence for both the Asker and the Giver. When the word "consequence" gets mentioned, people tend to think of its punitive connotations. I prefer to think of it as something that opens up or shuts down possibilities. The consequence of getting up late in the morning could be that you are late to work. Likewise, the consequence of getting up earlier could be that you are the first person in the office. The consequence of keeping your word could be that you get a bonus, and the consequence of not keeping your word could be that you don't. Consequences can be positive or negative. But even when negative, there is the opportunity to use them to learn and become more reliable at keeping your word in the future.

Appraise

Was the promise kept?

Having a clearly defined promise with measurements in place at the outset is critical if you're going to apply consequences. Once a promise puts a contract in place it's then either delivered or not. Assigning reward or some negative consequence in a situation where the promise is cloudy and its delivery vague will defeat your efforts to build accountability.

Consequences flow when the promise is clear-cut and its delivery – or non-delivery – clearly visible. When it is visible to both, then both feel more comfortable with the consequences. The answer to the question "Did you keep your promise?" must be a clear "yes" or "no." If it is a "yes," this clarity will be very satisfying for both you, the Asker, and the Giver. If it's a "no," check in with yourself before you begin to explore with the Giver the reasons why the promise wasn't kept. Stay above the line and ask the question, "Is there something that I have done, or failed to do, as the Asker, which may have resulted in this situation?" Askers tend to immediately blame the Giver, and usually there is learning to be had for both players.

> ### The outcome: the Asker's checklist
>
> 1. Did I make sure the Giver had a clearly defined goal and measures?
>
> 2. Did I discuss a tracking system so that we could keep score?
>
> 3. Did the Giver know what they had to do to keep the promise?
>
> 4. Did I train and coach them in their job?
>
> 5. Have I been willing to hold them to account and not accept excuses for non-performance which I felt could have been anticipated and mitigated?
>
> 6. Have I positively reinforced the desired behaviours by giving regular supportive feedback?

If you answer "no" to any of these questions, it may be that there is something for you to correct first. Take responsibility for your role in the delivery of the promise.

Getting to "why?"

Once you've completed the Asker's checklist, it's time to delve into the reasons why the promise wasn't kept. If the promise is a big one and the relationship one you want to preserve for the future, this is best done by video conference or face-to-face. For many Askers this is an uncomfortable conversation and they tend to not have it at all, or to have it by email. Hard though it is, looking someone in the eye while you have this conversation increases the likelihood it will be taken in a positive way. You don't want to get into blame or justification here, just stick to the facts and ask the question, "What happened?"

Common reasons for a promise not being delivered

- a "reasonable reason" or excuse which the Giver could have overcome

- an attitudinal problem: the Giver does not take accountability seriously, which has implications about whether they are the right person to ask to deliver something to you in the future

- a skill issue: the Giver (and probably you too) over-estimated the complexity of what was needed, and the Giver did not have the experience to fulfil this task. Next time training or additional support will be needed.

- a process issue: the Giver ran up against difficulties in how the promise was fulfilled. This is likely to cause the same difficulties next time unless the process is changed.

- an acceptable reason, which the Giver, in your opinion, could have done nothing to overcome

By identifying the reason, you'll be able to see which steps you need to take to correct the Giver's way of operating, or what consequences you need to apply. What you choose to do when a promise is not fulfilled is up to you. The most important thing of all is that you implement some form of consequence.

Considering consequences

You can apply a range of consequences when a promise isn't kept. These can run from having a chat with the Giver to see what they would do to correct things another time and make sure the same problem didn't happen again, to

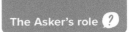

asking them to leave the organisation or deciding to end a business relationship. The only thing that won't work is doing nothing.

> **Tips for navigating consequences**
>
> 1. Let the Giver know you're aware that they didn't keep their word.
>
> 2. Let them know how you feel about that and the impact it has had on you.
>
> 3. Check whether they agree that a promise has been broken. Sometimes you may uncover misunderstandings about the exact nature of the promise.
>
> 4. Find out their ideas on how they can correct. If you accepted their "reasonable reasons," work out ways the Giver could operate differently next time, and how you could have both factored these "reasonable reasons" into the promise in the first place. Should the promise have only ever been seen as an intention, given such unforeseen circumstances were able to arise?

The persistent promise-breaker

If a person consistently breaks their word, have regular follow-up discussions with them. Use all the principles we have covered here including chunking the promise down into small steps and keeping the heat on.

Don't let non-performers get away with it over a period of time. If you don't do anything in response, it sends a message to others that accountability isn't important to you.

If all else fails, go back over "The outcome: the Asker's checklist" on page 80 once more. If you can honestly say that you have followed every part, then it may be time to question whether this is a person on whom you want to depend, whether they be a supplier or someone on your team.

Remember: if you're a boss and have people on your team who consistently fail to deliver promises, then your team will not be performing. As the boss, you are accountable for the sum total of your team's contributions. You can't afford to have one or more members of the team not pulling their weight long-term. If that person or those persons remain on your team and nothing changes, then you're avoiding the issue.

> In a robust accountability (promise) culture you have just cause for managing people out, should they prove to be consistent non-performers.

If you can show that time and again someone did not deliver, then the process of exiting them from the organisation will be much easier. Someone who does not keep his or her word will not, and should not, survive long in a highly accountable culture. Such exits serve to strengthen the culture for everyone else, because the leader is seen to be walking their talk.

As soon as poor performance is removed from the shadows, and all the usual hiding places of ambiguity, justification, "reasonable reasons" and procrastination have been removed, more often than not, poor performers will jump before they are pushed. It simply becomes too uncomfortable for them. Meanwhile, the achievers in your team will thrive.

🔍 CASE STUDY

A company to whom my colleagues and I were offering advice were pursuing an accountability culture, and as a result of a lot of work over three years felt they had achieved it to a large extent. Their ability to deliver what they promised had soared as a company, and at the individual level. The HR manager told me that about 10% of their people had come to him asking for support to find another job elsewhere. These people found the situation very stressful, missed how the culture had been before, and felt they did not fit. He was able to make this happen. The gaps were mostly filled by promoting younger people who were exceptional at keeping their word. The whole company experienced a refresh, and keeping your word became a challenge people embraced willingly, rather than something imposed.

Celebration

> ### Celebration is the positive consequence of keeping a promise.

The more people experience success, the more they believe they can achieve, and this momentum creates an unstoppable upward spiral. It's worth noting that lots of small celebrations have more impact than one annual one, even if that yearly celebration is big. Offering acknowledgement and recognition each time a promise is achieved has more impact

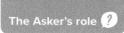

than one big bonus. This is true between two individuals, and in organisations.

To make sure your culture of promises is a positive and supportive one, it's important that both recognition and rewards are offered for promises kept. When you reward people frequently and publicly for keeping their word, it sends the signal that you are serious about promises. Rewards don't have to be monetary. For an achiever, some form of acknowledgement or thanks can be just as powerful as a financial reward or other recognition. For an exceptional promise delivered, a reward could be recognition of work in a public forum, selection for a special project, a request to mentor others, or a promotion. In the case of a supplier, it could of course be a request for more services. Acknowledgement of a promise kept confirms that the contract is complete, and it closes the loop on success.

Don't confuse effort with outcome. Rewarding effort without outcome should only happen in exceptional circumstances, where, for example, someone reached for a stretch goal which both of you had agreed was an intention, not a promise. In these circumstances, falling a little short but having taken risks which were worth stretching towards can itself be a rewardable event.

Any reward must be seen to be fair. If you reward those who don't keep promises equally to those who do, it makes a mockery of the promise and devalues it. You want to broadcast a message loud and clear that once a promise is made, it is made to be kept.

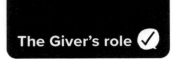
 Learn

Review

When a promise matters to you, and you fail to deliver, you will care very much. The way to overcome any sense of failure is to make sure that you learn from what happened, so you are able to improve your ability to make and keep promises in the future.

A promise can fail for a number of reasons, some of which may have occurred at the early stages before the promise was made, and some during the period after the promise. A characteristic of achievers who almost always keep their word is that they review dispassionately and thoroughly when a promise is not kept. Often, even when a promise is fulfilled, these people will review to consider whether they could have promised, and therefore achieved, more. This activity is initiated by you, as the Giver, perhaps completely independently of the Asker, although often reviews are done jointly.

A learning mindset

> If your mindset is a learning one, then the consequences of any promise can be positive, even if the promise doesn't get delivered.

First, you need to go above the line and take responsibility. It's easy to respond to failure with below-the-line responses

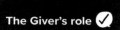

that are common in relationships and corporate cultures where the habits and skills of making and keeping promises are not embedded. Unfortunately, none of them contain the seeds of change required to master promises.

Here are some above-the-line alternatives to below-the-line statements that people often make when things go wrong:

Below the line	Above the line and looking for learning
"The original demand was unreasonable."	*"I knew it wasn't achievable and I didn't state my case strongly enough to the Asker. I just said "yes" anyway. Next time I will not make a promise unless I know it's achievable."*
"Things happened after I gave my word which I couldn't have predicted."	*"I need to get better at anticipating what might happen to cause me to break my word, so I can either give wiser promises or mitigate these things along the way."*
"I never really committed to the original request. It was imposed on me, and I didn't have any choice."	*"I made the choice to say I would do this, even though I had doubts at the time. I hoped things would work out and they didn't. In future I will only commit to demands that have been properly thought through by both sides."*
"People made new demands on me, and I couldn't do it all."	*"I wasn't able to negotiate well enough with multiple Askers so that all of them were satisfied. I need to prioritise my goals more effectively."*

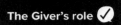

"I don't remember ever being clearly asked to do what I'm now being told I didn't deliver."	*"I heard a vague request, and I didn't follow up to see if the Asker was really serious. I didn't push them to define more closely what was being asked of me. In future I will always ask for clarification if I think a request is being made."*
"People are blaming me, but there are a whole lot of other people involved who are really at fault."	*"I wasn't successful at enrolling other key people so that we all pulled together to deliver on this promise. I need to negotiate interdependencies more effectively next time."*

The right-hand column has the language of the learner, of the person for whom the consequences of a failed promise provide rich learning experiences that will increase their skill at making wiser promises the next time around. People with this mindset master the skills of making and keeping promises over time and their reputation and trustworthiness grow accordingly. The responses in the left-hand column are those of people who are likely to be giving the same responses five years from now.

Celebration

You've kept your word, you're en route to becoming a woman or man of honour. If, as the well-known expression insists, "You are only as good as your word," you just got one notch better.

As we've learnt, high achievers are driven by intrinsic motivation. They are motivated by the desire to succeed, and their reward is success itself and the feeling of achievement. Making and keeping promises to colleagues provides them with a chance to feel this satisfaction.

A promise kept necessitates some form of internal celebration, as a minimum. While some celebration needs to be loud and public, often all that is required is a quiet acknowledgement of the affirmation you've made to yourself. A little clenched fist and a "yes." I watch sportspeople performing such personal acknowledgement rituals after a good shot or goal. Watch, learn and do the same.

Wins, however small, build self-esteem. A promise kept is a success because it is your success. The achievement of negotiating the right promise – one which is stretching enough to meet the demands of the Asker and show off all your talents, but not so demanding that the likelihood of success is low – can create a spiral of success which lifts esteem.

After the promise was made, in that period of time between commitment and fulfilment, you were able to navigate all the things that happened which could have knocked you off track. Things that other people will describe as "reasonable reasons" for not delivering on the promise were for you obstacles that you circumnavigated. You took your word seriously, and did not go below the line. You've proven yourself to be a person of your word. Something of great value in this world, and a cause for celebration indeed.

AFTERWORD

I n my years of working with many organisations, helping them build accountable cultures where giving and keeping your word is the norm, one company stand out as being absolutely exceptional. They bred accountability into everyone who worked there. They awakened the achievement motivation that most people have inside them. And as a result, it was a deeply satisfying place to be – fun, exciting, rewarding, trusting.

People didn't deliver because they had to, because they were afraid of what would happen to them if they didn't, or because delivering would earn them a bonus. They delivered because they wanted to, because the pleasure of stretching within such an environment far outweighed the effort that was required. People became empowered – not just because their bosses empowered them, but because everyone there had learnt that empowerment was something they could grab with two hands by promising and delivering, thereby building a reputation of trust between peers, and with their boss and their customers. Needless to say they were delivering incredible results, and they were the company everyone wanted to work for. They still are.

I have also met people who work for themselves whose high level of satisfaction with their work is based to a large extent on having built a reputation as someone who always delivers. In the absence of a large group around them, their reward is that quiet voice inside which says, "Yes, I did it," when they once again deliver what they said they would and see their client happy. I know others who work in difficult organisations and keep themselves sane by being able to make and keep their own promises, even while everyone around them fails to follow suit. Holding others to account in such organisations is not easy, because it is not the norm, but I know teams who are pockets of honour and reliability within a morass of avoidance and mistrust.

Suffice to say that accountability is achievable by anyone who puts their mind to it. And the rewards are personal, in terms of self-esteem and satisfaction, as well as financial, reputational and organisational. The journey to accountability is one which I strongly encourage you to pursue: refining your skills until you can say with confidence that your word really is your bond.

The @work series

The **@work** series is a collection of short, accessible and timely guides that convert culture goals into day-to-day practice, and help every aspiring leader to adopt more effective ways of working. Written by **Carolyn Taylor**, global expert in cultural excellence and transformational change, each title provides:

- Practical ways to improve how you work

- Advice on how to turn values into action and be seen as someone who walks their talk

- A road-map for encouraging different behaviour in those you work with

- Proven tools you can adopt and use with your team

Forthcoming titles include:

Courage@work
Simplicity@work
Trust@work
Inclusion@work
Empowerment@work
One-team@work

Available to order at: **info@carolyntaylorculture.com**

Or, to get details of when these titles will be available and to receive sample content and business insights, sign-up at: **https://carolyntaylorculture.com**

About the author

Photo: Dew Ariza

Carolyn Taylor is one of the world's foremost experts in organisational culture change and the Executive Chair of Walking the Talk **www.walkingthetalk.com**

During her 30 years in the field, Carolyn has run workshops with 200,000 leaders, worked alongside 200 culture change journeys, consulted on 15 mergers & acquisitions, and coached 60 CEOs, working in 35 countries.

She is the author of the classic text on culture change:

Walking the Talk: Building a Culture for Success
(revised edition, Penguin Random House, 2015)

"... a must read for any manager embarking on the journey of cultural change."

PROFESSOR LYNDA GRATTON, LONDON BUSINESS SCHOOL

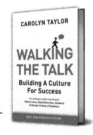

Carolyn hosts a regular podcast on leadership, authenticity and courage, available on iTunes, Spotify and other podcast platforms.

Reviews of Accountability@work

"This pocket-size book breaks down something incredibly complicated into simple steps that are easy for anyone to follow. It is so easy that you are left wondering why you aren't doing this already — but therein lies the magic of Carolyn's work, she has the art of making something very hard very do-able. I will definitely be buying this book for my team to ensure we drive the culture of accountability by adopting this approach."

CAROLINE BARTH, CHIEF HUMAN RESOURCES OFFICER AT LONZA

"Accountability is critical to the functioning of any business. Carolyn Taylor has spent years developing a road-map that allows you to create a scalable system of accountability. Packed with useful tips and advice, this is a must-read book for anyone who is involved in the business of making or keeping promises."

SIOBHAN McHALE, AUTHOR OF *THE INSIDER'S GUIDE TO CULTURE CHANGE*

In-house training programs, measurement tools and consulting advice – all based on the methodologies covered in Carolyn's books – are available through the consulting firm **Walking the Talk.**

Walking the Talk's mission is to make culture change do-able, so that organisations can achieve extraordinary business results through shaping the mindsets and behaviours of their people.

For more information, visit **walkingthetalk.com**

Carolyn is available for keynote presentations live or virtually. Contact her at:

https://carolyntaylorculture.com/

info@carolyntaylorculture.com

For more blogs, videos and commentary connect via LinkedIn

Linked in. **www.linkedin.com/in/carolyntaylorculture/**